Other Books by Leland Gregory

YOU BETCHA!

The **Witless** Wisdom
of Sarah Palin

Leland Gregory

**Andrews McMeel
Publishing, LLC**

Kansas City • Sydney • London

ISBN-13: 978-0-7407-9756-9
ISBN-10: 0-7407-9756-5

Library of Congress Control Number: 2010924912

10 11 12 13 14 RR2 10 9 8 7 6 5 4 3 2 1

www.andrewsmcmeel.com

Attention: Schools and Businesses

Andrews McMeel books are available at quantity discounts with bulk purchase
for educational, business, or sales promotional use. For information,
please write to: Special Sales Department, Andrews McMeel Publishing, LLC,
1130 Walnut Street, Kansas City, Missouri 64106.

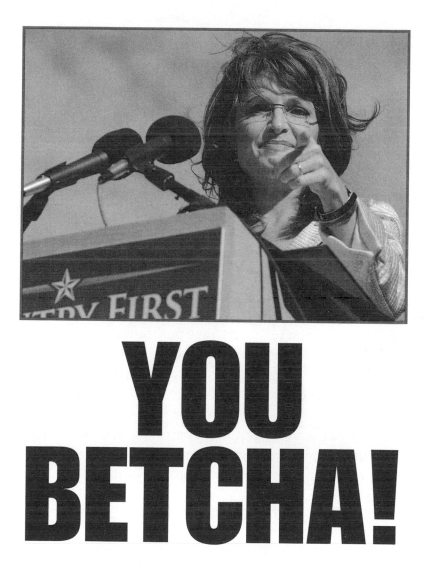

You Betcha!

"All of 'em, any of 'em that have been in front of me over all these years."

SARAH PALIN, UNABLE TO GIVE THE NAME OF ANY NEWSPAPER OR MAGAZINE SHE READS, IN AN INTERVIEW WITH KATIE COURIC, CBS NEWS, OCTOBER 1, 2008

★ ★ ★

"Because you're going to see anti-hunting, anti–Second Amendment circuses from Hollywood and here's how they do it. They use these delicate, tiny, very talented celebrity starlets, they use Alaska as a fund-raising tool for their anti–Second Amendment causes. Stand strong, and remind them patriots will protect our guaranteed individual right to bear arms, and, by the way, Hollywood needs to know, we eat, therefore we hunt."

GOVERNOR SARAH PALIN, RESIGNATION SPEECH, JULY 26, 2009, FAIRBANKS, ALASKA

You Betcha!

"**A**nd as for who coined that central war on terror being in Iraq, it was General Petraeus and al-Qaeda, both leaders there and it's probably the only thing that they're ever going to agree on, but that it was a central war on terror is in Iraq. You don't have to believe me or John McCain on that. I would believe Petraeus and the leader of al-Qaeda."

SARAH PALIN, VICE-PRESIDENTIAL DEBATE WITH SENATOR JOSEPH BIDEN, WASHINGTON UNIVERSITY, ST. LOUIS, MISSOURI, OCTOBER 2, 2008

 You Betcha!

"I've been touring this great, great land of ours over the last few weeks. I have to say, the view is much better from inside the bus, than under it!"

SARAH PALIN, GRIDIRON CLUB DINNER, DECEMBER 5, 2009, WASHINGTON, D.C.

5

You Betcha!

MASKED AVENGERS: This is Nicolas Sarkozy [the president of France] speaking. How are you?

SARAH PALIN: Oh, it's so good to hear you. Thank you for calling us.

MASKED AVENGERS: Oh, it's a pleasure.

SARAH PALIN: Thank you, sir, we have such great respect for you, John McCain and I. We love you and thank you for taking a few minutes to talk to me.

MASKED AVENGERS: I follow your campaigns closely with my special American adviser Johnny Hallyday, you know?

SARAH PALIN: Yes, good.

SÉBASTIEN TRUDEL AND MARC-ANTOINE AUDETTE, A CANADIAN COMEDY DUO KNOWN AS THE MASKED AVENGERS, PRANK PHONE CALL TO SARAH PALIN, ON THEIR SHOW, *LES CERVEAUX DE L'INFO,* ON CKOI-FM IN MONTREAL, NOVEMBER 1, 2008. JOHNNY HALLYDAY IS A ROCK-AND-ROLL LEGEND IN FRANCE.

You Betcha!

" [T]hey're in charge of the U.S. Senate so if they want to they can really get in there with the senators and make a lot of good policy changes that will make life better for Brandon and his family and his classroom."

SARAH PALIN, INCORRECTLY EXPLAINING THE VICE PRESIDENT'S
CONSTITUTIONAL ROLE AFTER BEING ASKED BY A THIRD GRADER
WHAT THE VICE PRESIDENT DOES, INTERVIEW WITH NBC AFFILIATE
KUSA IN COLORADO, OCTOBER 21, 2008

★ ★ ★

"Perhaps so."

SARAH PALIN, ASKED BY CHARLIE GIBSON IF AMERICA MAY NEED
TO GO TO WAR WITH RUSSIA BECAUSE OF THE GEORGIA CRISIS,
ABC NEWS INTERVIEW, SEPTEMBER 11, 2008

"Sometimes, you know, I consider myself, too, as a feminist, whatever that means."

SARAH PALIN, INTERVIEW WITH GRETA VAN SUSTEREN,
ON THE RECORD, NOVEMBER 10, 2008

★ ★ ★

"Now like a lot of you, perhaps, I have spent the last year thinking about how to best serve. How can I help our country? How can I make sure that I, that you, that we're in a position of nobody being able to succeed?"

SARAH PALIN, TEA PARTY CONVENTION,
NASHVILLE, TENNESSEE, FEBRUARY 6, 2010

You  Betcha!

"Well, it was an unfair attack on the verbiage that Senator McCain chose to use. The fundamentals that he was having to explain afterward, he means the work force, he means ingenuity of the American people. And, of course, that is strong, that is the foundation of our economy. So that was an unfair attack based on verbiage that John McCain used. Certainly, it is a mess, though."

SARAH PALIN, IN AN INTERVIEW WITH SEAN HANNITY,
ON WHY IT WASN'T FAIR TO USE JOHN MCCAIN'S OWN WORDS AGAINST HIM,
FOX NEWS, SEPTEMBER 17, 2008

"Carmex. I'm addicted to Carmex. I don't go anywhere without Carmex."

SARAH PALIN, *ESQUIRE* INTERVIEW, MARCH 2009

★ ★ ★

"That's a healthy thing. That means my perspective is fresher."

SARAH PALIN, EXPLAINING WHY HAVING NO NATIONAL EXPERIENCE AND LESS THAN TWO YEARS' EXPERIENCE AS A GOVERNOR IS A POSITIVE THING, *TIME* MAGAZINE INTERVIEW, AUGUST 29, 2008

You Betcha!

SARAH PALIN: Nice to meet you.
JOE BIDEN: It's a pleasure.
SARAH PALIN: Hey, can I call you Joe?

VICE-PRESIDENTIAL DEBATE BETWEEN SENATOR JOSEPH BIDEN
AND GOVERNOR SARAH PALIN, WASHINGTON UNIVERSITY,
ST. LOUIS, MISSOURI, OCTOBER 2, 2008

★ ★ ★

"Before I became governor of the great state of Alaska, I was mayor of my hometown. And since our opponents in this presidential election seem to look down on that experience, let me explain to them what the job involves.

I guess a small-town mayor is sort of like a 'community organizer,' except that you have actual responsibilities."

SARAH PALIN, ACCEPTANCE SPEECH, 2008 REPUBLICAN NATIONAL CONVENTION,
XCEL ENERGY CENTER, ST. PAUL, MINNESOTA, SEPTEMBER 3, 2008

You Betcha!

"They're our next-door neighbors and you can actually see Russia from land here in Alaska, from an island in Alaska."

SARAH PALIN, EXPLAINING HER VIEWS ON FOREIGN RELATIONS WITH RUSSIA, ABC NEWS INTERVIEW, SEPTEMBER 11, 2008

★ ★ ★

"In what respect, Charlie?"

SARAH PALIN, AFTER BEING ASKED BY CHARLIE GIBSON IF SHE AGREED WITH THE BUSH DOCTRINE, ABC NEWS INTERVIEW, SEPTEMBER 11, 2008

You  Betcha!

MASKED AVENGERS: Yes, you know we have a lot in common also, because except from my house I can see Belgium. That's kind of less interesting than you.

SARAH PALIN: Well, see, we're right next door to different countries that we all need to be working with, yes.

SÉBASTIEN TRUDEL AND MARC-ANTOINE AUDETTE, A CANADIAN COMEDY DUO KNOWN AS THE MASKED AVENGERS, PRANK PHONE CALL TO SARAH PALIN, ON THEIR SHOW, *LES CERVEAUX DE L'INFO,* ON CKOI-FM IN MONTREAL, NOVEMBER 1, 2008

You  Betcha!

"I had an interview with John Ziegler on his new radio show and he asked me about a comment that, uh, Letterman had made regarding my appearance as a 'slutty flight attendant' and I, and, my first thought was, hey, don't disparage flight attendants."

SARAH PALIN, INTERVIEW WITH MATT LAUER, ON NBC'S *TODAY* SHOW, JULY 12, 2009

"Left Unalakleet warmth for rain in Juneau tonite. No drought threat down here, ever but consistent rain reminds us: 'No rain? No rainbow!'"

SARAH PALIN, TWEET, JULY 2009

"How about that amazing closing ceremony [of the Winter Olympics]. It was beautiful. The minute I saw the giant moose, I remembered I hadn't cooked anything for the kids' dinner."

SARAH PALIN, *THE TONIGHT SHOW WITH JAY LENO*,
MARCH 2, 2010

★ ★ ★

"I've been so focused on state government, I haven't really focused much on the war in Iraq."

SARAH PALIN, INTERVIEW WITH *ALASKA BUSINESS MONTHLY*,
MARCH 2007

You  Betcha!

"What's the differencc between a pit bull and a hockey mom? Lipstick."

SARAH PALIN, ACCEPTANCE SPEECH, 2008 REPUBLICAN NATIONAL CONVENTION, XCEL ENERGY CENTER, ST. PAUL, MINNESOTA, SEPTEMBER 3, 2008

QUESTION: "Are you offended by the phrase 'under God' in the Pledge of Allegiance? Why or why not?"

SARAH PALIN: "Not on your life. If it was good enough for the founding fathers, it's good enough for me and I'll fight in defense of our Pledge of Allegiance."

ANSWER TO A 2006 QUESTIONNAIRE FOR ALASKA'S GUBERNATORIAL RACE. THE PLEDGE WAS WRITTEN IN 1892 AND THE WORDS "UNDER GOD" WERE NOT ADDED UNTIL JUNE 14, 1954.

"Absolutely. Yup, yup. Especially with a good team around us."

ASKED BY *PEOPLE* MAGAZINE, "DO YOU FEEL READY TO BE A HEARTBEAT AWAY FROM THE PRESIDENCY?" THIS WAS AFTER PALIN WAS CHOSEN TO RUN FOR VICE PRESIDENT, AUGUST 2008.

★ ★ ★

"God truly has shed his grace on thee—on this country. He's blessed us, and we better not blow it."

SARAH PALIN, ABC NEWS INTERVIEW, APRIL 20, 2010

You  Betcha!

"She sounds chipper and annoyingly nasal, so I realize now why people think she's me. Ugh."

SARAH PALIN, DENYING THAT IT WAS HER VOICE HEARD ON TELEPHONE ROBOCALLS FOR LISA MURKOWSKI'S 2004 U.S. SENATE CAMPAIGN AGAINST TONY KNOWLES, *ANCHORAGE DAILY NEWS*, OCTOBER 24, 2006

★ ★ ★

"How's that hope-y, change-y stuff workin' out for ya?"

SPEAKING TO OBAMA SUPPORTERS IN NASHVILLE, TENNESSEE, AT A GATHERING OF TEA PARTY ACTIVISTS, ASSOCIATED PRESS, FEBRUARY 8, 2010

You Betcha!

"And you know, small mayors, mayors of small towns, quote unquote. They're on the front lines."

Hannity & Colmes, FOX News, September 19, 2008

★ ★ ★

"It is obvious to me who the good guys are in this one and who the bad guys are.

The bad guys are the ones who say Israel is a stinking corpse, and should be wiped off the face of the earth. That's not a good guy."

Sarah Palin, interview with Katie Couric,
CBS News, September 25, 2008

You Betcha!

"So, if I went off script once in a while, I can't for the life of me remember any one time where it would have harmed him [John McCain], or the ticket. So I don't regret it."

SARAH PALIN, FORGETTING HER MANY BOTCHED INTERVIEWS AND RAMBLING, INCOHERENT SPEECHES, INTERVIEW WITH GRETA VAN SUSTEREN, *ON THE RECORD,* NOVEMBER 10, 2008

MASKED AVENGERS: Governor Palin, I love the documentary they made on your life. You know, *Hustler*'s *Nailin' Paylin?*

SARAH PALIN: Oh, good, thank you, yes.

SÉBASTIEN TRUDEL AND MARC-ANTOINE AUDETTE, A CANADIAN COMEDY DUO KNOWN AS THE MASKED AVENGERS, REFERRING TO *HUSTLER*'S HARD-CORE PORNOGRAPHIC FILM, *WHO'S NAILIN' PAYLIN?*, WHICH STARRED A SARAH PALIN LOOK-ALIKE, NOVEMBER 1, 2008

You Betcha!

"I think on a national level your Department of Law there in the White House would look at some of the things that we've been charged with and automatically throw them out."

SARAH PALIN, REFERRING TO A GOVERNMENTAL DEPARTMENT THAT DOES NOT EXIST, ABC NEWS INTERVIEW, JULY 7, 2009

You Betcha!

"And first, some straight talk for some, just some in the media because another right protected for all of us is freedom of the press, and you all have such important jobs reporting facts and informing the electorate, and exerting power to influence. You represent what could and should be a respected, honest profession that could and should be the cornerstone of our democracy. Democracy depends on you, and that is why, that's why our troops are willing to die for you. So, how 'bout in honor of the American soldier, ya quite makin' things up."

GOVERNOR SARAH PALIN, RESIGNATION SPEECH,
JULY 26, 2009, FAIRBANKS, ALASKA

"We used to hustle over the border for health care we received in Canada. And I think now, isn't that ironic?"

SARAH PALIN, ADMITTING HER FAMILY USED TO GET TREATMENT IN CANADA, WHICH HAS THE TYPE OF SOCIALIZED MEDICINE THAT SHE HAS FOUGHT AGAINST IN THE UNITED STATES, MARCH 6, 2010

You  Betcha!

"It's kind of what Reagan used to do, though, when he used to talk about, say, the Evil Empire. You're never going to find 'the Evil Empire' on a map of the world. He talked about that in terms that people could understand. . . . Now, had he been criticized and mocked and condemned for using a term that wasn't actually there on a map or in documents, we probably would have never succeeded in quashing the Evil Empire and winning that."

SARAH PALIN, INTERVIEW WITH BARBARA WALTERS,
NOVEMBER 18, 2009

"**O**ne of my absolute best friends for the last thirty years happens to be gay and I love her dearly, and she is not my 'gay' friend, she is one of my best friends, who happens to have made a choice that isn't a choice that I have made, but . . . I'm not gonna judge people."

SARAH PALIN, INTERVIEW WITH KATIE COURIC, CBS NEWS, OCTOBER 1, 2008

★ ★ ★

"It is good to be here and in front of this audience of leading journalists and intellectuals. Or, as I call it, a death panel."

SARAH PALIN, GRIDIRON CLUB DINNER, DECEMBER 5, 2009, WASHINGTON, D.C.

"So the things that he has done right now as president in protecting the country, more power to him. We appreciate that he kind of went there fully with the commanders on the ground asking for more reinforcements in Afghanistan. Couldn't get there all the way with these guys, but kind of went there. Good, more power to you."

SARAH PALIN, INTERVIEW WITH CHRIS WALLACE, *FOX NEWS SUNDAY*, FEBRUARY 7, 2010

 You Betcha!

"Who calls a shot like that? Who makes a decision like that? It's a disturbing trend."

Sarah Palin (West Allis, Wisconsin, November 6, 2009), promoting a conspiracy theory that the Obama administration had moved "In God We Trust" to the edge of U.S. coins. The change was actually made in 2005 during the Bush administration and was reversed by Congress as part of the Consolidated Appropriations Act of 2008. Obama didn't take office until January 20, 2009.

"They are also building schools for the Afghan children so that there is hope and opportunity in our neighboring country of Afghanistan."

SARAH PALIN, GIVING A FUND-RAISING SPEECH IN SAN FRANCISCO, OCTOBER 5, 2008

★ ★ ★

"How sad that Washington and the media will never understand; it's about country. And though it's honorable for countless others to leave their positions for a higher calling and without finishing a term, of course we know by now, for some reason a different standard applies for the decisions I make."

SARAH PALIN, FACEBOOK POST, JULY 4, 2009

"It may be tempting and more comfortable to just keep your head down, plod along, and appease those who demand: 'Sit down and shut up,' but that's the worthless, easy path; that's a quitter's way out."

SARAH PALIN, ANNOUNCING HER RESIGNATION AS GOVERNOR,
JULY 3, 2009

"Let me go back to a comfortable analogy for me—sports . . . basketball. I use it because you're naive if you don't see the national full-court press picking away right now: A good point guard drives through a full-court press, protecting the ball, keeping her eye on the basket . . . and she knows exactly when to pass the ball so that the team can *win*."

SARAH PALIN, ANNOUNCING HER RESIGNATION AS GOVERNOR,
JULY 3, 2009

"Hot? If only people could see me as I come in from a run early in the morning without a trough full of makeup on, I think that they'd have a different opinion."

SARAH PALIN, *ESQUIRE* INTERVIEW, MARCH 2009

★ ★ ★

"Letterman certainly has the right to 'joke' about whatever he wants to, and thankfully we have the right to express our reaction. This is all thanks to our U.S. military women and men putting their lives on the line for us to secure America's right to free speech—in this case, may that right be used to promote equality and respect."

SARAH PALIN, MISINTERPRETING THE FIRST AMENDMENT, IN A STATEMENT TO FOXNEWS.COM, JUNE 16, 2009

"It's great to see another part of the country."

SARAH PALIN, CAMPAIGNING IN PENNSYLVANIA, AUGUST 30, 2008

★ ★ ★

"I can't claim a Bill Clinton and say that I never inhaled."

SARAH PALIN, ON HER ADMISSION OF USING MARIJUANA, WHICH WAS LEGAL UNDER ALASKA STATE LAW EVEN THOUGH IT WAS ILLEGAL UNDER U.S. LAW, *ANCHORAGE DAILY NEWS*, AUGUST 6, 2006

You Betcha!

"**O**K, we're confident that we're going to win on Tuesday, so from there, the first hundred days, how are we going to kick in the plan that will get this economy back on the right track and really shore up the strategies that we need over in Iraq and Iran to win these wars?"

SARAH PALIN, IMPLYING THAT WE ARE AT WAR WITH IRAN, FOX NEWS INTERVIEW, NOVEMBER 1, 2008

★ ★ ★

"I'm the mayor. I can do whatever I want until the courts tell me I can't."

SARAH PALIN, AS QUOTED BY FORMER CITY COUNCIL MEMBER NICK CARNEY, AFTER HE RAISED OBJECTIONS ABOUT THE $50,000 SHE SPENT RENOVATING THE MAYOR'S OFFICE WITHOUT APPROVAL OF THE CITY COUNCIL, *SALON*, SEPTEMBER 14, 2008

 You Betcha!

"I would hope at least that those protesters have the courage and the honor of thanking our veterans for giving them the right to protest!"

SARAH PALIN, TO SUPPORTERS AT A CAMPAIGN RALLY
WHO HAD SHOUTED "WE CAN'T HEAR YOU!" AND "LOUDER!"
RICHMOND, VIRGINIA, OCTOBER 13, 2008

★ ★ ★

"I'll try to find you some and I'll bring them to you."

SARAH PALIN, ASKED BY KATIE COURIC TO SUPPORT HER CLAIM THAT
JOHN MCCAIN HAS PUSHED FOR MORE REGULATION IN HIS TWENTY-SIX YEARS
IN THE SENATE, CBS NEWS INTERVIEW, SEPTEMBER 24, 2008

You Betcha!

"**I** watched with the volume all the way down. I thought it was hilarious. I thought she was spot on. . . . It was hilarious. Again, didn't hear a word she said, but the visual, spot on."

Sarah Palin, on Tina Fey's *SNL* skit during an interview on FOX News's *Hannity & Colmes*, September 17, 2008

★ ★ ★

"**C**ertainly, accounting for different conditions in that different country and conditions are certainly different."

Sarah Palin, vice-presidential debate with Senator Joseph Biden, Washington University, St. Louis, Missouri, October 2, 2008

★ ★ ★

"**A**s for that VP talk all the time, I'll tell you, I still can't answer that question until somebody answers for me what is it exactly that the VP does every day?"

Sarah Palin, after U.S. presidential candidate John McCain chose her as his vice-presidential running mate, interview with CNBC's *Kudlow & Co*, July 31, 2008

You Betcha!

"We'll keep clinging to our Constitution and our guns and our religion. You can keep the change."

SARAH PALIN, AT THE TEA PARTY EXPRESS, BOSTON, MASSACHUSETTS,
APRIL 15, 2010

"It's great to be on the same show as Shaun White. Last time I was this close to the Flying Tomato was when someone threw one at me at a book signing."

SARAH PALIN, *THE TONIGHT SHOW WITH JAY LENO*, MARCH 2, 2010

★ ★ ★

"The secret to chili is you gotta have good mooseburger in there. I don't know if you can get moose commercially in New York. You'd have to come up here and visit me in my home, and I'll prepare it for ya."

SARAH PALIN, *ESQUIRE* INTERVIEW, MARCH 2009

MASKED AVENGERS: Well, I hope for you. You know, we have a lot in common because personally one of my favorite activities is to hunt, too.

SARAH PALIN: Oh, very good. We should go hunting together.

MASKED AVENGERS: Exactly, we could try to go hunting by helicopter like you did. I never did that. Like we say in French, *on pourrait tuer des bébé phoques aussi* (we can kill baby seals, also).

SÉBASTIEN TRUDEL AND MARC-ANTOINE AUDETTE, A CANADIAN COMEDY DUO KNOWN AS THE MASKED AVENGERS, PRANK PHONE CALL TO SARAH PALIN, ON THEIR SHOW, *LES CERVEAUX DE L'INFO,* ON CKOI-FM IN MONTREAL, NOVEMBER 1, 2008

"I don't want to say that the U.S. government is taking over the role of the private sector, but I have to admit, on the flight here, thumbing through a magazine and looking at a photo of President Obama with the president of China, the person next to me pointed at it and said, 'Hu's a communist.' I thought they were asking a question."

SARAH PALIN, GRIDIRON CLUB DINNER, DECEMBER 5, 2009, WASHINGTON, D.C.

★ ★ ★

"Earth saw clmate chnge4 ions;will cont 2 c chnges.R duty2responsbly devlop resorces4humankind/not pollute&destroy;but cant alter naturl chng"

SARAH PALIN, TWEET, DECEMBER 19, 2009

"You can't blink. You have to be wired. In a way of being so committed to the mission, the mission that we're on, reform of this country, and victory in the war, you can't blink. So I didn't blink."

SARAH PALIN, INTERVIEW WITH CHARLIE GIBSON,
ABC NEWS, SEPTEMBER 11, 2008

★ ★ ★

"A little advice to Tina Fey– I want to make sure she's holding on to that Sarah outfit. Because she's gonna need it in the next four years."

SARAH PALIN, COLUMBUS, OHIO, NOVEMBER 2, 2008

You Betcha!

"Nah, absolutely not necessarily."

SARAH PALIN, WHEN ASKED BY MATT LAUER IF SHE IS THE FUTURE OF THE GOP, NBC'S *TODAY* SHOW, JULY 12, 2009

★ ★ ★

"Let me speak specifically about a credential that I do bring to this table, Charlie, and that's with the energy independence that I've been working on for these years as the governor of this state that produces nearly 20 percent of the U.S. domestic supply of energy."

SARAH PALIN, EXAGGERATING THE AMOUNT OF ENERGY PRODUCED BY ALASKA, WHICH IS ONLY 3.5 PERCENT, INTERVIEW WITH CHARLIE GIBSON, ABC NEWS, SEPTEMBER 11, 2008

"**B**arack Obama and Senator O'Biden, you've said no to everything in trying to find a domestic solution to the energy crisis that we're in."

SARAH PALIN, VICE-PRESIDENTIAL DEBATE WITH SENATOR JOSEPH BIDEN, WASHINGTON UNIVERSITY, ST. LOUIS, MISSOURI, OCTOBER 2, 2008

★ ★ ★

"**H**ello. Thank you, Jay. Thank you. I'm so happy to get to be here. This is a thrill of a lifetime really. And Alaska, being so different from Los Angeles. Here when people have a frozen look on their face, I find out it's BOTOX."

SARAH PALIN, *THE TONIGHT SHOW WITH JAY LENO*, MARCH 2, 2010

"You know what I thought they were going to come after me for? Getting a D in a college course twenty-two years ago. That was the big controversy in my little world. That was the skeleton in my closet. Crap. Once the media finds that out . . ."

SARAH PALIN, INTERVIEW WITH BILL O'REILLY,
FOX NEWS, NOVEMBER 19, 2009

You  Betcha!

"Joe the Plumber and as we talked about today in the speech, too, he's representing, you know, Jane the Engineer, and Molly the Dental Hygienist, and Chuck the Teacher and, and all these good, hardworking Americans who are, finally, were able to hear in very plain talk the other night, what Barack Obama's intentions were to redistribute wealth."

SARAH PALIN, INTERVIEW WITH DREW GRIFFIN,
CNN, OCTOBER 21, 2008

"You travel this road in life and as you turn a corner and there may be something there that circumstances change, you've got to call an audible and you decide to shift gears, take another direction. I'm always open for that."

SARAH PALIN, CNN INTERVIEW WITH WOLF BLITZER,
NOVEMBER 12, 2008

★ ★ ★

"I don't waste a lot of time watching TV and doing some things that maybe that some other people would do."

SARAH PALIN, INTERVIEW WITH SEAN HANNITY,
HANNITY & COLMES, FOX NEWS, SEPTEMBER 18, 2008

You  Betcha!

"They are kooks, so I agree with Rush Limbaugh. Rush Limbaugh was using satire. . . . I didn't hear Rush Limbaugh calling a group of people whom he did not agree with 'f-ing retards,' and we did know that Rahm Emanuel, as has been reported, did say that. There is a big difference there."

SARAH PALIN, ON WHY IT WAS ALL RIGHT FOR LIMBAUGH TO USE THE WORD "RETARDS" BUT NOT EMANUEL, *FOX NEWS SUNDAY* INTERVIEW, FEBRUARY 7, 2010

"This is what I always do. I'm like, OK, God, if there is an open door for me somewhere, this is what I always pray, I'm like, don't let me miss the open door. Show me where the open door is. Even if it's cracked up a little bit, maybe I'll plow right on through that and maybe prematurely plow through it, but don't let me miss an open door."

SARAH PALIN, INTERVIEW WITH GRETA VAN SUSTEREN,
ON THE RECORD, NOVEMBER 10, 2008

You Betcha!

"What would America do w/out FOX News?I'm so thankful for the opportunity to work w/team committed to fair&balanced reporting.Please join us!"

SARAH PALIN, TWEET, JANUARY 11, 2009

You  Betcha!

"Profiles in Courage, they can be hard to come by these days. You know, so often we just find them in books. But next week when we nominate John McCain for president, we're putting one on the ballot."

SARAH PALIN, McCAIN CAMPAIGN EVENT, DAYTON, OHIO, AUGUST 29, 2008. *PROFILES IN COURAGE* IS A 1957 PULITZER PRIZE–WINNING BIOGRAPHY WRITTEN BY JOHN F. KENNEDY.

You  Betcha!

"Because, Katie, you're not the center of everybody's universe. Maybe that's why they didn't think to ask that question among so many other things to be asked."

SARAH PALIN, RESPONDING TO KATIE COURIC'S APPEARANCE ON *THE LATE SHOW WITH DAVID LETTERMAN*, WHEN COURIC QUESTIONED WHY THE MEDIA DIDN'T FOLLOW UP WITH PALIN'S INABILITY TO RESPOND TO WHAT NEWSPAPERS SHE READS, INTERVIEW WITH JOHN ZIEGLER, JANUARY 5, 2009, WASILLA, ALASKA

"We want to see Ivana [Trump] because we are so desperate in Alaska for any semblance of glamour and culture."

SARAH PALIN, APRIL 3, 1996, *ANCHORAGE DAILY NEWS*

★ ★ ★

"Canada needs to dismantle its public health-care system and allow private enterprise to get involved and turn a profit."

SARAH PALIN, SHORTLY BEFORE BEING ASKED NOT TO ATTEND
A HOSPITAL FUND-RAISER IN TORONTO, CANADA, *TORONTO SUN*,
DECEMBER 18, 2009

"And then in the summertime such extreme summertime, about 150 degrees hotter than just some months ago, than just some months from now, with fireweed blooming along the frost heaves and merciless rivers that are rushing and carving and reminding us that here, Mother Nature wins. It is as throughout all Alaska that big wild good life teeming along the road that is north to the future. That is what we get to see every day."

GOVERNOR SARAH PALIN, RESIGNATION SPEECH, JULY 26, 2009, FAIRBANKS, ALASKA

★ ★ ★

"Only dead fish go with the flow."

SARAH PALIN, ANNOUNCING HER RESIGNATION AS GOVERNOR, JULY 3, 2009

KATIE COURIC: What other Supreme Court decisions do you disagree with?

SARAH PALIN: Well, let's see. There's—of course—in the great history of America rulings there have been rulings, there's never going to be absolute consensus by every American. And there are—those issues, again, like *Roe v. Wade* where I believe are best held on a state level and addressed there. So you know—going through the history of America, there would be others but—

KATIE COURIC: Can you think of any?

SARAH PALIN: Well, I could think of—of any again, that could be best dealt with on a more local level. Maybe I would take issue with. But you know, as mayor, and then as governor and even as a vice president, if I'm so privileged to serve, wouldn't be in a position of changing those things but in supporting the law of the land as it reads today.

CBS NEWS INTERVIEW, OCTOBER 1, 2008

MASKED AVENGERS: Yes, yes, I understand we have the equivalent of Joe the Plumber in France. It's called Marcel, the guy with bread under his armpit.

SARAH PALIN: Right, that's what it's all about, the middle class and government needing to work for them. You're a very good example for us here.

SÉBASTIEN TRUDEL AND MARC-ANTOINE AUDETTE, A CANADIAN COMEDY DUO KNOWN AS THE MASKED AVENGERS, PRANK PHONE CALL TO SARAH PALIN, ON THEIR SHOW, *LES CERVEAUX DE L'INFO*, ON CKOI-FM IN MONTREAL, NOVEMBER 1, 2008

"I didn't really have a good answer, as so often—is me. But then somebody sent me the other day, Isaiah 49:16, and you need to go home and look it up. Before you look it up, I'll tell you what it says though. It says, hey, if it was good enough for God, scribbling on the palm of his hand, it's good enough for me, for us. He says, in that passage, 'I wrote your name on the palm of my hand to remember you,' and I'm like, 'OK, I'm in good company.'"

SARAH PALIN, COMMENTING ON THE FACT THAT SHE HAD NOTES WRITTEN ON HER HAND DURING HER TEA PARTY CONVENTION SPEECH, MARCH 5, 2010

"From my hotel room, from there I can see the Russian Embassy, right there."

SARAH PALIN, GRIDIRON CLUB DINNER, DECEMBER 5, 2009,
WASHINGTON, D.C.

★ ★ ★

"Great day w/bear management wildlife biologists; much to see in wild territory incl amazing creatures w/mama bears' gutteral raw instinct to protect & provide for her young; She sees danger? She brazenly rises up on strong hind legs, growls Don't Touch My Cubs & the species survives & mama bear doesn't look 2 anyone else 2 hand her anything; biologists say she works harder than males, is provider/protector for the future." (Palin's tweet continues.) "Yes it was another outstanding day in AK seeing things the rest of America should see; applicable life lessons we're blessed to see firsthand."

JULY 15, 2009

You  Betcha!

"It's nice to get out and do something to promote a local business and to just participate in something that isn't so heavy handed politics that it invites criticism. Certainly we'll probably invite criticism for even doing this, too, but at least this was fun."

AFTER PARDONING A TURKEY FOR THANKSGIVING, SARAH PALIN CONDUCTED AN INTERVIEW WITH WASILLA TELEVISION STATION KTUU, WHILE OTHER TURKEYS WERE SLAUGHTERED IN THE BACKGROUND, NOVEMBER 20, 2008

★ ★ ★

"[Tax] dollars go to projects that have little or nothing to do with the public good–things like fruit-fly research in Paris, France. I kid you not."

SARAH PALIN, REFERRING TO A $211,000 USDA STUDY SEEKING WAYS TO BETTER CONTROL *BACTROCERA OLEAE*, THE OLIVE FRUIT FLY, IN MONTPELLIER, FRANCE, WHICH IS HARMFUL TO AMERICAN AGRICULTURE, SPEECH IN PITTSBURGH, PENNSYLVANIA, OCTOBER 24, 2008

"And man, just these everyday hardworking Americans whom we would meet. And again, such a comfort that we had knowing that we aren't the only ones believing in America being the land of possibilities and opportunity, but the federal government, man, it's got to play its appropriate role—not get in the way of the progress of our families and our businesses—and for their example and their love, too."

SARAH PALIN, GRAND JUNCTION, COLORADO,
OCTOBER 21, 2008

"**S**till, when I see this administration in action, I can't help think of what might have been. I could be the vice president overseeing the signing of bailout checks. And Joe Biden would be on the road, selling his new book, *Going Rogaine*."

SARAH PALIN, GRIDIRON CLUB DINNER,
DECEMBER 5, 2009, WASHINGTON, D.C.

"The point is, though, that we have lost millions and millions and millions of jobs as we have incurred greater and greater debt and deficit. . . . The bailouts, the takeovers of the private sector—that's not the answer. That is not what built this great country into the most prosperous, healthiest, safest country on Earth."

SARAH PALIN, CONTRADICTING HERSELF WITHIN SECONDS DURING AN INTERVIEW WITH CHRIS WALLACE, *FOX NEWS SUNDAY*, FEBRUARY 7, 2010

You Betcha!

"They see some of the idiosyncrasies of the personalities who control the political machines and they don't want to waste time dealing with that, so they are independent, but they are believers in the [Tea Party] movement and I think you're going to see a whole lot of the Independents and more conservative Democrats finally be empowered and emboldened and say, yes, I'll come out of the closet now and I'll let them know I believe in it, too."

SARAH PALIN, Q & A AFTER TEA PARTY CONVENTION SPEECH,
NASHVILLE, TENNESSEE, FEBRUARY 6, 2010

"**O**il and coal? Of course, it's a fungible commodity and they don't flag, you know, the molecules, where it's going and where it's not. But in the sense of the Congress today, they know that there are very, very hungry domestic markets that need that oil first. So, I believe that what Congress is going to do, also, is not to allow the export bans to such a degree that it's Americans that get stuck to holding the bag without the energy source that is produced here, pumped here. It's got to flow into our domestic markets first."

SARAH PALIN, WHO JOHN MCCAIN CLAIMED TO BE THE NATION'S
FOREMOST EXPERT ON ENERGY, SPEAKING OFF THE CUFF AT A
TOWN HALL MEETING, GRAND RAPIDS, MICHIGAN, SEPTEMBER 17, 2008

You Betcha!

"And getting up here I say it is the best road trip in America soaring through nature's finest show. Denali, the great one, soaring under the midnight sun. And then the extremes. In the wintertime it's the frozen road that is competing with the view of ice-fogged frigid beauty, the cold, though, doesn't it split the Cheechakos from the Sourdoughs?"

GOVERNOR SARAH PALIN, RESIGNATION SPEECH,
JULY 26, 2009, FAIRBANKS, ALASKA

You Betcha!

"He [Barack Obama] not understanding that no, we don't want to just chill a li'l bit, and cool a little bit on his health care plan. We want the thing killed because it's government takeover of about one-sixth of our economy."

SARAH PALIN, FOX NEWS, JANUARY 28, 2010

★ ★ ★

"We North Americans, we come from the stock of our ancestors."

SARAH PALIN, SPEECH AT CARMEN'S BANQUET HALL IN
HAMILTON, ONTARIO, CANADA, BENEFITING CHARITY OF HOPE,
GLOBE AND MAIL, APRIL 16, 2010

"OK, today is a beautiful day and today as we swear in Sean Parnell, no one will be happier than I to witness by God's grace Alaskans with strength of character advancing our beloved state. Sean has that."

GOVERNOR SARAH PALIN, RESIGNATION SPEECH, JULY 26, 2009, FAIRBANKS, ALASKA

 You Betcha!

"Copenhgen=arrogance of man2think we can change nature's ways.MUST b good stewards of God's earth,but arrogant&naive2say man overpwers nature"

SARAH PALIN, TWEET, DECEMBER 19, 2009

You Betcha!

"**If** [the media] convince enough voters that that is negative campaigning, for me to call Barack Obama out on his associations, then I don't know what the future of our country would be in terms of First Amendment rights and our ability to ask questions without fear of attacks by the mainstream media."

SARAH PALIN, REVERSING THE TRUE MEANING OF FIRST AMENDMENT RIGHTS WHILE SUGGESTING THAT CRITICISM OF HER IS UNCONSTITUTIONAL, RADIO INTERVIEW WITH CHRIS PLANTE, WMAL-AM, OCTOBER 31, 2008

You  Betcha!

"I may not answer the questions that either the moderator or you want to hear, but I'm going to talk straight to the American people and let them know my track record, also."

SARAH PALIN, ON NOT ANSWERING THE QUESTIONS IN THE
VICE-PRESIDENTIAL DEBATE WITH SENATOR JOSEPH BIDEN,
WASHINGTON UNIVERSITY, ST. LOUIS, MISSOURI, OCTOBER 2, 2008

"**A**s Putin rears his head and comes into the air space of the United States of America, where–where do they go? It's Alaska. It's just right over the border. It is–from Alaska that we send those out to make sure that an eye is being kept on this very powerful nation, Russia, because they are right there. They are right next to–to our state."

SARAH PALIN, IN AN INTERVIEW WITH KATIE COURIC, EXPLAINING HOW ALASKA'S PROXIMITY TO RUSSIA GIVES HER FOREIGN POLICY EXPERIENCE, CBS NEWS, SEPTEMBER 24, 2008

You  Betcha!

"**W**ell, it certainly does because our—our next-door neighbors are foreign countries. They're in the state that I am the executive of. And there in Russia. . . . We have trade missions back and forth. We—we do— it's very important when you consider even national security issues with Russia."

SARAH PALIN, IN AN INTERVIEW WITH KATIE COURIC, FORGETTING THAT OUR TWO NEXT-DOOR NEIGHBORS ARE ACTUALLY CANADA AND MEXICO, CBS NEWS, SEPTEMBER 24, 2008

You  Betcha!

"**B**ut, ultimately, what the bailout does is help those who are concerned about the health care reform that is needed to help shore up our economy. Um, helping, oh, it's got to be about job creation, too. Shoring up our economy, and putting it back on the right track. So health-care reform and reducing taxes and reining in spending has got to accompany tax reductions, and tax relief for Americans, and trade—we have got to see trade as opportunity, not as, uh, competitive, um, scary thing, but one in five jobs created in the trade sector today. We've got to look at that as more opportunity. All of those things under the umbrella of job creation."

SARAH PALIN, EXPLAINING GEORGE BUSH'S $700 BILLION GOVERNMENT BAILOUT OF WALL STREET TO KATIE COURIC, CBS NEWS INTERVIEW, SEPTEMBER 24, 2008

You  Betcha!

"That's exactly what we're going to do in a Palin and McCain administration."

SARAH PALIN, POSITIONING HERSELF AT THE TOP OF THE PRESIDENTIAL TICKET, CEDAR RAPIDS, IOWA, SEPTEMBER 18, 2008

★ ★ ★

"The fact is that Fannie Mae and Freddie Mac have gotten too big and too expensive to the taxpayers."

SARAH PALIN, DEMONIZING TWO COMPANIES, WHICH ARE IN FACT PRIVATE ENTITIES, COLORADO SPRINGS, COLORADO, SEPTEMBER 13, 2008

"**Y**ou are a cynic. Because show me where I have ever said that there's absolute proof that nothing that man has ever conducted or engaged in, has had any effect, or no effect, on climate change."

SARAH PALIN, IN AN INTERVIEW WITH CHARLIE GIBSON,
ABC NEWS, SEPTEMBER 11, 2008

You Betcha!

"A changing environment will affect Alaska more than any other state, because of our location. I'm not one, though, who would attribute it to being man-made."

SARAH PALIN, DISMISSING THE LINK BETWEEN GLOBAL WARMING AND HUMAN ACTIVITY, NEWSMAX INTERVIEW, AUGUST 2008

You  Betcha!

"**P**ray for our military men and women who are striving to do what is right. Also, for this country, that our leaders, our national leaders, are sending soldiers out on a task that is from God. That's what we have to make sure that we're praying for, that there is a plan and that that plan is God's plan."

SARAH PALIN, EXPLAINING TO STUDENTS AT THE WASILLA ASSEMBLY OF GOD CHURCH THAT CONTINUING THE WAR IN IRAQ IS GOD'S PLAN, JUNE 2008

★ ★ ★

"I told the Congress, 'Thanks, but no thanks,' on that Bridge to Nowhere."

SARAH PALIN, IN HER ACCEPTANCE SPEECH AT THE 2008 REPUBLICAN NATIONAL CONVENTION, XCEL ENERGY CENTER, ST. PAUL, MINNESOTA, SEPTEMBER 3, 2008, FORGETTING THAT SHE FOUGHT FOR THE GRAVINA ISLAND BRIDGE BEFORE SHE WAS AGAINST IT

BILL O'REILLY: Let me be very bold and fresh again. Do you believe that you are smart enough, incisive enough, intellectual enough to handle the most powerful job in the world?

SARAH PALIN: I believe that I am because I have common sense and I have, I believe, the values that I think are reflective of so many other American values, and I believe that what Americans are seeking is not the elitism, the um, the ah, a kind of spineless, spinelessness that perhaps is made up for that with some kind of elite, Ivy League education and, and a fat résumé that is based on anything but hard work and private sector, free enterprise principles. Americans are could be seeking something like that in positive change in their leadership. I'm not saying that that has to be me.

NOVEMBER 19, 2009, FOX NEWS, *THE O'REILLY FACTOR*

You Betcha!

KATIE COURIC: You've cited Alaska's proximity to Russia as part of your foreign policy experience. What did you mean by that?

SARAH PALIN: That Alaska has a very narrow maritime border between a foreign country, Russia, and, on our other side, the land boundary that we have with Canada. It's funny that a comment like that was kinda made to . . . I don't know, you know . . . reporters.

KATIE COURIC: Mocked?

SARAH PALIN: Yeah, mocked, I guess that's the word, yeah.

CBS NEWS, SEPTEMBER 25, 2008

You  Betcha!

"**Y**ou mentioned education, and I'm glad that you did. I know education you are passionate about with your wife being a teacher for thirty years, and God bless her. Her reward is in heaven, right?"

SARAH PALIN, REFERRING TO JOE BIDEN'S WIFE, JILL, DURING THE VICE-PRESIDENTIAL DEBATE, WASHINGTON UNIVERSITY, ST. LOUIS, MISSOURI, OCTOBER 2, 2008

★ ★ ★

"**B**ut I will tell Americans straight up that I don't support defining marriage as anything but between one man and one woman, and I think through nuances we can go round and round about what that actually means."

SARAH PALIN, VICE-PRESIDENTIAL DEBATE WITH SENATOR JOSEPH BIDEN, WASHINGTON UNIVERSITY, ST. LOUIS, MISSOURI, OCTOBER 2, 2008

"**N**o, in fact, when we talk about the Bush administration, there's a time, too, when Americans are going to say, 'Enough is enough with your ticket,' on constantly looking backward, and pointing fingers, and doing the blame game."

SARAH PALIN, WHILE THE BUSH ADMINISTRATION WAS STILL IN CONTROL, DURING THE VICE-PRESIDENTIAL DEBATE WITH SENATOR JOSEPH BIDEN, WASHINGTON UNIVERSITY, ST. LOUIS, MISSOURI, OCTOBER 2, 2008

You  Betcha!

Sarah Palin: Well, I think we could have a lot of fun together while we're getting work done. We can kill two birds with one stone that way.

Masked Avengers: I just love killing those animals. Mmm, mmm, take away life, that is so fun. I'd really love to go, so long as we don't bring along Vice President Cheney.

Sarah Palin: No, I'll be a careful shot, yes.

Sébastien Trudel and Marc-Antoine Audette, a Canadian comedy duo known as the Masked Avengers, prank phone call to Sarah Palin, on their show, *Les Cerveaux de l'Info,* on CKOI-FM in Montreal, November 1, 2008

"And I just say bless you. And you guys are just a bunch of cool-looking Christians also. Ben, I don't know you well yet, but looking at you I bet people are thinking they're going to be interested in Jesus Christ through you because of the way you look: this redheaded Sasquatch for Jesus! You look good!"

SARAH PALIN, MASTER'S COMMISSION OF WASILLA, ALASKA,
JUNE 8, 2008

You Betcha!

"I don't know if you're going to use the word 'terrorist' there."

SARAH PALIN, ASKED IF PEOPLE WHO BOMB ABORTION CLINICS ARE TERRORISTS, NBC NEWS INTERVIEW, OCTOBER 23, 2008

★ ★ ★

"I have not, and I think if you go back in history and if you ask that question of many vice presidents, they may have the same answer that I just gave you."

SARAH PALIN, AFTER BEING ASKED IF SHE HAD EVER MET A FOREIGN HEAD OF STATE, APPARENTLY UNAWARE THAT EVERY VICE PRESIDENT IN THE LAST THIRTY-TWO YEARS HAD MET A FOREIGN HEAD OF STATE PRIOR TO TAKING OFFICE, ABC NEWS INTERVIEW WITH CHARLIE GIBSON, SEPTEMBER 11, 2008

"And how long have I been at this, like five weeks? So there hasn't been a whole lot that I've promised."

SARAH PALIN, VICE-PRESIDENTIAL DEBATE WITH SENATOR JOSEPH BIDEN, WASHINGTON UNIVERSITY, ST. LOUIS, MISSOURI, OCTOBER 2, 2008

"The next morning we drove to John McCain's ranch in Sedona. John was waiting on the porch. Before he can say a word, I tell him, I'm quoting now. 'I know why I'm here, and I'm ready. But, I'm worried. The cost of credit protection for the largest U.S. banks is rising precipitously. Have you given any thought to the run on the entities in the parallel banking system? Do you realize the vulnerability created when these institutions borrow short term in liquid markets to invest long term in illiquid assets?' John said, 'You betcha!' I thought, 'You betcha?' Who talks that way?"

SARAH PALIN, GRIDIRON CLUB DINNER, DECEMBER 5, 2009,
WASHINGTON, D.C.